THE BRITISH AIRMAN
OF THE
SECOND WORLD WAR

Stuart Hadaway

SHIRE PUBLICATIONS

Published in Great Britain in 2013 by Shire Publications Ltd, Midland House, West Way, Botley, Oxford OX2 0PH, United Kingdom.

44-02 23rd Street, Suite 219, Long Island City, NY 11101, USA.

E-mail: shire@shirebooks.co.uk   www.shirebooks.co.uk

© 2013 Stuart Hadaway.

A CIP catalogue record for this book is available from the British Library.

Shire Library no. 728.   ISBN-13: 978 0 74781 222 7

Stuart Hadaway has asserted his right under the Copyright, Designs and Patents Act, 1988, to be identified as the author of this book.

Designed by Tony Truscott Designs, Sussex, UK and typeset in Perpetua and Gill Sans.

Printed in China through Worldprint Ltd.

13 14 15 16 17   10 9 8 7 6 5 4 3 2 1

COVER IMAGE
Supermarine Spitfire pilots from No. 40 Squadron, South African Air Force. (IWM TR 1033)

TITLE PAGE IMAGE
Supermarine Spitfire pilot Flying Officer W. R. B. McMurray, No. 241 Squadron, in Italy. (IWM TR 1540)

CONTENTS PAGE IMAGE
Supermarine Spitfire pilots of No. 222 Squadron at RAF North Weald. (IWM COL 192)

ACKNOWLEDGEMENTS
I would like to thank for their help: Nina Hadaway, David Hadaway, David Buttery, Lewis Shelley, Colin Foster and the Harder Family, Tim Newark, and Vernon Creek.

PICTURE ACKNOWLEDGEMENTS
Isabel Butler, page 23; Vernon Creek, pages 19, 21 and 27; Harder family, pages 5 (right), 31, 35 (top), 38 (bottom) and 42; Imperial War Museum, cover image, title page, contents page, pages 8 (both), 11, 12, 16, 22, 24, 28 (both), 29, 30, 31 (top), 35 (bottom), 36, 38 (top), 41, 44, 45, 47, 48, 49 and 58–9; Mark Murphy, page 18 (top); Peter Newark Picture Library, pages 4, 15, 39, 43 and 50; William Potter, page 60; Raymond Rees, page 46; Lewis Shelley, pages 13, 18 (bottom), 20, 34 and 37; Mark Stefanicki, page 40; and Richard Willis, page 61.

IMPERIAL WAR MUSEUM COLLECTION
Many of the photos in this book come from the Imperial War Museum's huge collections which cover all aspects of conflict involving Britain and the Commonwealth since the start of the twentieth century. These rich resources are available online to search, browse and buy at www.iwmcollections.org.uk. In addition to Collections Online, you can visit the Visitor Rooms where you can explore over 8 million photographs, thousands of hours of moving images, the largest sound archive of its kind in the world, thousands of diaries and letters written by people in wartime and a huge reference library. To make an appointment, call (020) 7416 5320, or e-mail mail@iwm.org.uk. Website: www.iwm.org.uk

Shire Publications is supporting the Woodland Trust, the UK's leading woodland conservation charity, by funding the dedication of trees.

CONTENTS

INTRODUCTION

DURING the Second World War, the men and women of Britain's air forces served all over the world. The operations they flew, the aircraft they operated, and the conditions and environments in which they lived varied so drastically that this book can only be a brief introduction to what they experienced. It will give an insight into some of the common threads that bound together Britain's airmen and airwomen, and provide a taste of what they endured while playing their vital part in the eventual victory.

Opposite: Hawker Hurricanes on the cover of a *Boy's Own* magazine, March 1941.

Above: A pilot of No. 64 Squadron poses with his proud rigger and fitter. As these two ground crew maintained and prepared his aircraft, his life would be in their hands.

Left: A de Havilland Mosquito of No. 109 Squadron, high over Germany.

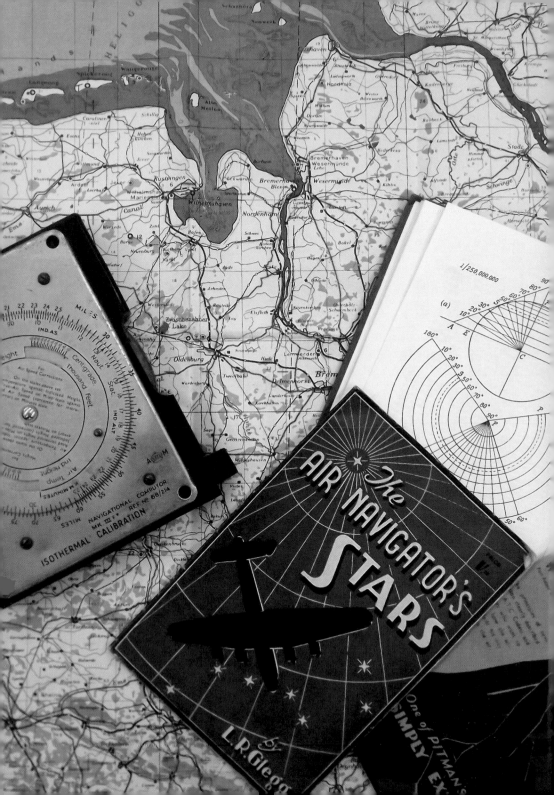

MAKING AN AIRMAN

EARLY IN THE WAR, most aircrew would receive their trade and flying training in Britain, often being sent to front-line squadrons to complete the final stages before becoming 'operational'. This system was unsuitable for producing the massive numbers needed in wartime, and sending half-trained crews to operational squadrons was soon halted. It became clear that no-one there had the time or energy to look after these ill-prepared fledglings, and casualty rates among them were unacceptably high.

As the war progressed, training programmes expanded and lengthened as further needs were identified, more complicated aircraft introduced, or specialisations developed. Sometimes it was simply a case that, early on, as many aircrew as possible were needed straight away; only later was the luxury of time available. For example, in 1939 the average pilot had undergone thirty to thirty-six weeks of flying training. By 1944, heavy bomber pilots were receiving courses eighty-one to eighty-five weeks long (with up to 464 hours in the air), and fighter pilots seventy to seventy-two weeks (up to 360 hours in the air). Depending on the types of aircraft and operations that a navigator was training for, by 1944 he could expect to train for between sixty-three and eighty-one weeks as he mastered different equipment.

For ground crews, ever more complicated technology meant that greater degrees of specialisation were needed, with airmen becoming more focused on particular pieces of kit. Interestingly, this worked the other way with airwomen. Initially, members of the Women's Auxiliary Air Force were trained for very specific tasks (such as changing spark plugs) as it was believed they did not have the technical aptitude for more complicated tasks. Time showed that they did, though, and gradually the WAAF became less specialised, and they received training in broader roles.

It should also be emphasised that, although at times qualified personnel in some trades were in very short supply, the RAF never compromised on its technical training, and the highest standards were expected and maintained throughout the war.

Opposite: Navigation was a rapidly developing science, and students needed good maths skills. Manuals, tables and basic computers all helped with training and operations.

New recruits
taking a
Morse Code test
at the Aircrew
Reception Centre,
St John's Wood.
(IWM CH 7518)

SELECTION AND INITIAL TRAINING

Aircrew consistently suffered the highest British casualty rates throughout
the Second World War. Bomber crews would on average survive just seven
operations, and some other types such as torpedo bomber crews at times

New members
of the Women's
Auxiliary Air Force
being kitted out
in Chiswick.
(IWM CH 2584)

Far left: Cadet (later Sergeant) John Hadaway on leave, showing the distinctive white cap flash of the aircrew cadet.

Left: A sergeant pilot. One in three aircrew were commissioned on finishing their training, the rest becoming non-commissioned officers. However, around a quarter of those NCOs would later receive commissions, making the average balance between officer and NCO aircrew 50:50.

had even lower life expectancies than that. Every single member of RAF aircrew was, and had to be, a volunteer. In fact for much of the war the willingness to volunteer overcame other considerations; for example, one of the very few ways for a civilian in a reserved occupation to join the regular armed forces was to volunteer for aircrew.

After registering with the local recruiting office, prospective aircrew would wait to be called to a test centre for evaluation. Early in the war this meant medical assessment and an interview panel, but as the war dragged on a whole series of physical and psychometric tests was devised and perfected to assess individuals. These would separate the candidates into the aircrew categories to which they were most suited, and identify those who would be unlikely to make the grade.

Candidates would then be summoned to an Aircrew Reception Centre, the most famous of which was in Regent's Park, London. This site not only included Lord's Cricket Ground and London Zoo, but also Winfield House, which was owned by Barbara Hutton, the Woolworth's heiress and wife of Cary Grant; it is now the residence of the US Ambassador. After signing on, being kitted out, and receiving further medical examinations (and, to the dismay and discomfort of most, multiple inoculations and vaccinations), the new recruits would then be posted to Initial Training Wings (ITW).

These were often based in coastal resorts, where the war had left many empty boarding houses and hotels that could be used as billets, empty theatres and music halls for use as lecture theatres, and open esplanades which made ideal drill squares, to the amusement of holiday-makers. Here recruits would receive basic training in military life, and their first instruction in the mysteries of their designated trade. Tests at the end of ITW would whittle out those who had not reached the required standards. These personnel would be 'back-flighted' to retake the course, or after several failures re-mustered into other trades. Those who passed would proceed to the next level of training, which for pilots meant attending Elementary Flying Training Schools. Here they would reach the standard of 'going solo'. As with the trade tests, this would ensure that nobody who was unsuitable would be sent overseas and put through further expensive training, thus saving valuable money and resources.

TRAINING OVERSEAS

The majority of RAF aircrew trained overseas, where the skies were safer and direct enemy intervention unlikely (although the risks of getting there over U-boat infested waters remained). Convoys of troopships transported thousands of cadets at a time across the Atlantic, or down the coast of Africa. Cramped and highly uncomfortable, with sometimes questionable standards of rations, these ships were a marked contrast to their final destinations. In an age when few people ever travelled overseas, the vast, wide-open spaces

An intake of No. 8 Initial Training Wing pose on the esplanade at Newquay.

of the Canadian and American prairies, or the South African veldt, were an awe-inspiring sight, while standards of living were often considerably higher than those they had left behind. In North America in particular, and especially before the United States entered the war, the availability of food and luxury goods was a cause of celebration. Eventually, the Air Ministry began to put size and frequency limits on the mail their cadets were sending home, because of the number of parcels being sent that were packed with rare or rationed goods (not only did this practice create logistical strains in shipping the parcels, it also raised morale issues at home).

There were several overseas schemes, the main ones being:

- British Flying Training Schools (BFTS): six schools in the US which trained around 7,000 pilots from 1941–5.
- The Arnold Scheme: run by the United States Army Air Force, produced nearly 4,400 pilots from 1941–3.
- The Towers Scheme: run by the US Navy, and trained 1,800 pilots, 540 navigators and 660 wireless operators from 1941–2.
- The Pan America Scheme: navigation training provided by PanAm Airways, which produced 1,200 navigators from 1940–2.

Training Wireless Operators of No. 10 (Signals) Recruits Centre, in the Olympia Exhibition Hall, the Winter Gardens, Blackpool. (IWM CH 2039)

- The British Commonwealth Air Training Scheme (also known as the Riverdale Agreement, or Dominion Air Training Scheme): this Canadian scheme produced around half of all RAF pilots, about 138,000 British, Canadian, Australian or New Zealand personnel, from 1939 to 1945.
- The Rhodesian Air Training Group, which ran from 1939–41, alongside the Van-Brookham Agreement from 1940, before being combined into the Joint Air Training Scheme from 1941. These Rhodesian and South African schemes produced some 36,000 British, South African or Australian aircrew.

Many other Dominion aircrew were trained through the expansion of their own air forces; for example, 28,000 men were trained by the Royal Australian Air Force and 6,500 were trained by the Royal New Zealand Air Force.

Working as a crew required close teamwork, but crews usually only met in the very last weeks of training.

OPERATIONAL TRAINING

Most aircrew then finished their training in Britain. Usually, current operational types of aircraft were not sent overseas; nor was the most up-to-date technical equipment, such as radars or electronic warfare sets. The latest kit was often in short supply, and none could be spared to be shipped off

for training purposes. Instead, it remained in Britain, where it could be diverted for operational use if necessary. By introducing crews to their final aircraft types in the UK, they would also get used to flying them in the dreary and inhospitable northern European skies that most would have to operate in. Having trained so far in America, Canada or South Africa, heavy clouds or fog would be alien to many of them. Perhaps even more daunting, they would also have to learn to navigate over landscapes that were entirely blacked-out at night.

Even in a fighter, the number of dials, switches and levers that had to be learnt to the point of instinctive understanding and location was daunting.

As well as being introduced to their aircraft, most personnel would also be introduced to the rest of their crews at this stage. 'Crewing up' occurred at Operational Training Units (OTUs). Sometimes crews were simply assigned, but more often a suitable number of personnel to form a set number of crews would be brought together, and sometimes in the course of an afternoon but more commonly over a few days or even weeks, left to sort themselves into working crews. Letting each crew pick itself was far more efficient than arbitrarily forcing them together.

A lot of crews would attend further advanced training after OTU, for example in glider towing. Bomber crews in particular went through various conversion units or 'finishing schools', as even at OTU level they were usually flying obsolete and battle-worn aircraft. Despite this, as part of the OTU course they would often take part in a handful of operations, dropping leaflets over France, laying mines off Holland, or sometimes, when they were needed to make up numbers, taking part in main force operations over Germany. For the first Thousand Bomber raid, on Cologne in May 1942, of the 1,047 aircraft involved, 365 were from OTUs. Interestingly, the OTUs (many crewed by instructors) suffered the same casualty rate as the main force crews.

GROUND CREWS

Trainee ground crew were sent to a Recruits Centre for three to five days of kit issue, orientation and testing for their prospective trades. From there, they were also sent to ITWs, for courses which by mid-1943 were standardised as eight weeks for men and three weeks for women. Here they learned the basic military arts, procedures and law, as well as undergoing further trade testing and evaluation. At the end of the course, they would be despatched to a trade school. There were over two hundred of these, scattered around the country. Some were on formal RAF camps, such as the Wireless Schools at RAF Yatesbury, while others were in requisitioned buildings or even contracted out to civilian schools.

It would be impossible to trace the process for every trade; there were forty-one ground trades in the RAF in 1939, but this grew to over 350 by 1944, and the courses changed continually. In 1942 alone, Technical Training Command promulgated some 700 official changes to their syllabi. Some of these changes were considerable, and could cause significant backlogs. Airmen would be posted to menial jobs on RAF stations, or even sent home, while the system straightened itself out. Sometimes these kinks worked all the way back to Recruits Centres, who would enlist men and women and then send them straight home again.

Courses were intensive and concentrated, but also highly efficient, covering subjects in months that would take years in civilian life. Long hours

The coveted winged brevet of a qualified Pilot. Underneath is the log book which every member of aircrew had to maintain, recording all of their flying.

Airmen's skills needed constant practice even after training. Posters, such as this one for aircraft identification, or for emergency procedures, were displayed in crew rooms to act as constant reminders.

and regular tests ensured a high standard was achieved. Once basic trade training had been completed, and final tests passed, the ground crews would be posted to active stations and units as fully qualified 'erks'. But their education would not end there. Advanced training as well as courses on new equipment and operational procedures would follow, and all promotion was based on passing stringent trade tests.

OPERATIONAL

PEOPLE GATHERED from across the UK, the Dominions and Empire, occupied Europe (including Germans and Austrians, mostly Jews) and the rest of the free world to serve with the RAF in the Second World War. Some squadrons were 'owned' by particular countries, such as the Polish, Czechoslovakian and Free French units; others were linked to countries such as Rhodesia, America or parts of India. Some were simply attached to the RAF from the Royal Australian, Royal New Zealand or South African Air Forces. The Royal Canadian Air Force sent enough units to make up an entire Bomber Group, No. 6. While these units maintained national characteristics, most in fact contained a mix of personnel, and a crew could contain as many nationalities as there were positions. In fact, the RAF was far more cosmopolitan than their cultural image would have us expect. Take the classic, clipped BBC tones used by aircrew in popular culture: in the 1940s, regional accents were much stronger than today, so a certain middle ground had to be found so that men from Manchester, Ontario,

Opposite:
The Wireless Operator's station on a Vickers Warwick transport aircraft from No. 525 Squadron. This was more open than most heavy aircraft, and the cabin heat vent was just by their feet so it was also warmer than on most too.
(IWM CH 12931)

AIR GUNNER
PILOT
AIR GUNNER
FLIGHT ENGINEER
AIR GUNNER
WIRELESS OPERATOR/AIR GUNNER
BOMB AIMER
NAVIGATOR

Left; Crew positions on a Handley Page Halifax.

17

Right: The cramped cockpit of a Bristol Blenheim, where the Pilot and Observer would sit, while the Bomb Aimer's position can be seen through the hatch on the right.

Below:
A re-enactor sits in a Supermarine Spitfire cockpit. Notice the cravat: a good fighter pilot would keep his head constantly turning, searching the sky, and the cravat would stop his collar from rubbing.

Jamaica, Glasgow and London could all understand each other over a crackly intercom system.

PILOTS

Even though the Pilot might not be the most senior ranking crewmember, in the air they were the 'skipper' and in command. As captain of the aircraft, in almost all circumstances (see Air Bomber on page 24) they had the final say in the fate and actions of their aircraft and crew. Even if they had no crew to take responsibility for, the prospect of commanding an aeroplane could be daunting. Battle of Britain pilot Anthony Bartley DFC recalled his conversion to single-seat fighters:

'One of the unique and most alarming experiences in one's life must surely be to find oneself alone in an aeroplane … completely dependent upon oneself to get back to mother earth.'

Flying different types of aircraft required distinct skills and temperaments, and, although it was possible to retrain later, potential pilots were sorted at a very early stage in their training into those destined for single-engined and those for multi-engined aircraft. Fighter pilots had to have quick reactions,

The surprisingly restrictive cockpit of a Douglas Dakota transport aircraft.

A re-enactor
in the cramped
bubble of a
Supermarine
Spitfire cockpit.

good eyesight and (preferably) an aggressive streak. They also had to be able to undertake some serious multi-tasking, navigating and operating the wireless while flying. Coastal and Bomber pilots had to have a more dogged and patient attitude to fly, and concentrate, for many hours at a time. With the large four-engined aircraft, physical strength was also needed.

NAVIGATORS

In 1939, Navigators (and Air Bombers and Wireless Operators) were all grouped together under the generic title 'Observers', but this belittled both their roles and their skills. By 1942, each trade was separated out, and indeed different types of Navigator began to be recognised as well. The type of Navigator varied with the type of aircraft, and the kinds of equipment used in them. The equipment used made great leaps forward during the war, from simple slide-rules and sextants in 1939, to radar, radio-beams and rudimentary analogue computers by 1945; it has been, very accurately, stated that navigation rose from being an art form in 1939, to being a science by 1945. Whereas only around 23 per cent of heavy bombers came within three miles of their targets in early 1942, the introduction of radio-beams such as Gee and radar such as H2S increased that figure to 95 per cent by 1945. These complex, and secret, gadgets were not usually allowed out of the country for training, and so Navigators learned their art the old-fashioned way, using maps, stars and dead reckoning, before being introduced to the latest science only in the last stages of their training, back in the UK. While on operations, they would go through a constant cycle of checks, using (it was advised) at least three different methods in order to cross-check the accuracy of their plotting. Navigators in smaller aircraft also trained to act as Wireless Operators and Air Bombers, and to operate air-to-air radar. However, in such aircraft

Opposite:
The cockpit
area of an Avro
Lancaster. The
Navigator's table
is at foreground
left, with his
various 'boxes of
tricks' above. The
Pilot and Flight
Engineer were to
the front, and the
Wireless Operator
immediately
behind the
Navigator.

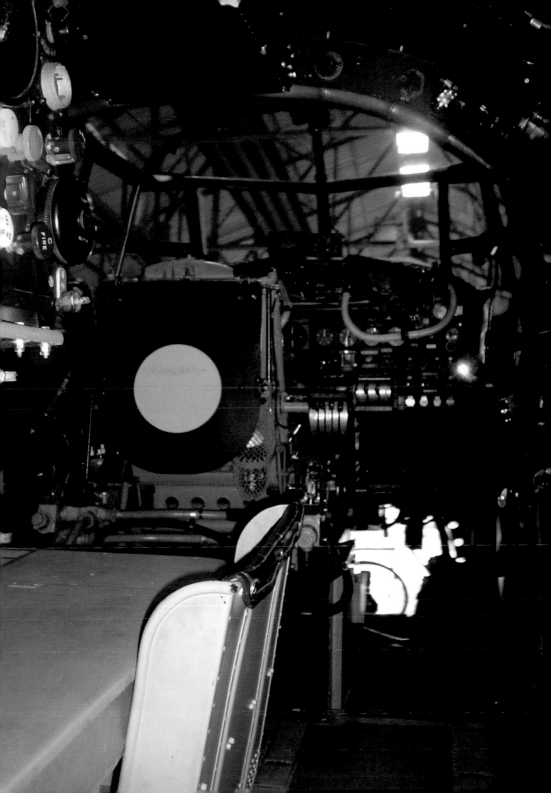

there was sometimes no room for anything but very basic kit. Dave McIntosh DFC was a Navigator on Mosquito intruders:

A Navigator using a sextant in the astrodome of a Vickers Wellington. At night, star sightings would be made through the same dome to help plot positions. (IWM CH 475)

In practice, our navigation on 418 Squadron boiled down to this: we took a long pencil and marked it off in inches. Each inch was four miles or one minute. The pencil laid between two points on the map gave us the rough course and the notches in it gave us the time and distance. We only had three basic tools: the pencil, the map, and the flashlight to see the map. That was in the air. On the ground, you worked out as much basic information as you could with proper compass and ruler. But as soon as your pilot went hurrying off after an enemy plane or a train or a convoy, all that prepared stuff was out as you were left with the three original basics.

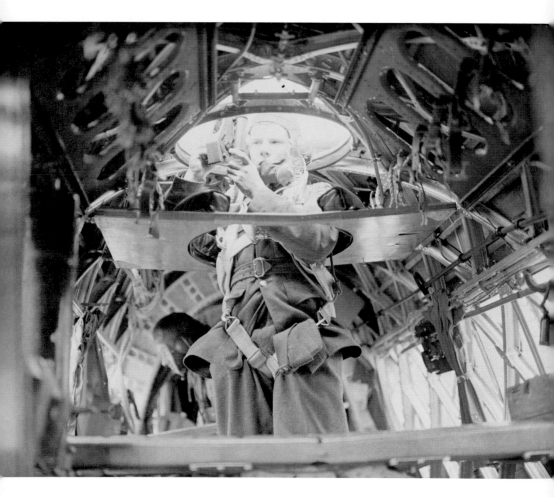

WIRELESS OPERATORS

The Wireless Operator (W/Op) was responsible for maintaining contact with the ground, and potentially other aircraft. Early in the war, most W/Ops also trained as Air Gunners, and were expected to man a turret as well. When the larger four-engined aircraft were introduced, the emphasis on gunnery slipped somewhat. These aircraft were powerful enough to carry men to act just as gunners, freeing up the W/Op to concentrate on his duties. Often this simply meant monitoring communications from home, or from other aircraft out on patrol, due to the restrictions placed on broadcasting signals that the enemy could use to calculate positions and send fighters to intercept, although this restriction mainly applied to bombers flying over enemy territory. However, contact, damage and progress reports could be made as the flight progressed, usually transmitted in Morse Code. Some navigational aids would also be monitored or relayed by the W/Op, and later they would use systems that could jam German signals.

Like the Navigator, the W/Op would spend the bulk of their time huddled over their equipment at their crew station, seeing only their tiny corner of the aircraft as they monitored their equipment. Being surrounded by all of their electrical equipment would at least have the effect of keeping them warm at higher altitudes.

Wireless Operator/Air Gunner Sergeant Sydney Swallow, kitted out in padded suit, fur-lined boots and hefty gloves. He was killed while training in December, 1942.

FLIGHT ENGINEERS

Flight Engineers were partly the product of the increasing complexity of aircraft as the war dragged on. In the early years of the war, it was common practice for bombers and other long-range aircraft to carry two pilots: the second pilot, or 'second dickie' was often just out of training, and their role (apart from gaining experience) was to help the Pilot monitor the aircraft's engines and systems, while also relieving them if they were wounded or nature called. If no second pilots were available, a ground engineer was often carried instead.

A Flight Engineer on his folding seat in the cockpit of an Avro Lancaster, leaning back to monitor the instruments for the engines.
(IWM CH 12289)

This system was wasteful of valuable Pilots and unfair on the engineers who acted without official recognition. As aircraft became more complicated it was clear a new specialist was needed. In 1942, the trade of Flight Engineer was recognised. Their task was to sit or crouch, often in very cramped and uncomfortable conditions, in the cockpit with the Pilot. They monitored the instruments and adjusted the controls for the engines, fuel consumption, hydraulics and various other systems, and could potentially even repair damaged or failing systems. They would also have basic flight training, and be able to take over if the Pilot needed a break, or was wounded. By 1944, these tasks required no less than fifty-three weeks of training.

AIR BOMBER

Air Bomber (also known as Bomb Aimer) was another trade to grow out of the 'Observer' class, due to the increasing complexity of their task. For most of the flight they would help out around the aircraft, taking sightings

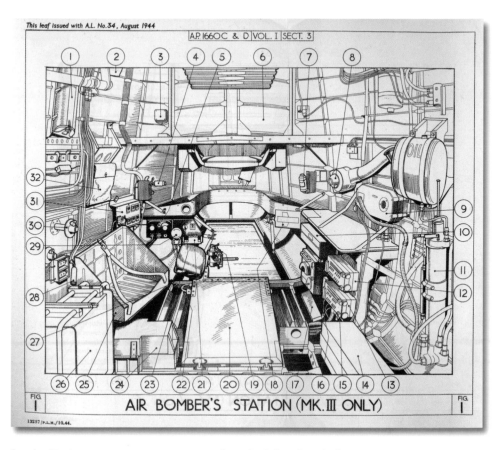

This leaf issued with A.L. No.34, August 1944

A.P. 1660C & D VOL. I SECT. 3

AIR BOMBER'S STATION (MK.III ONLY)

FIG. I

FIG. I

13257/P.L.N./10.44.

for the Navigator, manning a turret, or aiding the Pilot (for which some received basic flight training). However, their principal role was concerned with perhaps the briefest but most important part of any sortie: the attack on a target.

During an attack, Air Bombers had to make sure that their sights were set up correctly (with up-to-date wind directions and strengths, and to account for the aerodynamics of the bomb types being used) and that the correct bombs and sequences were selected on their Bomb Selector panel. Once the technical side was set, the Air Bomber would (through verbal commands to the Pilot) take control of the aircraft, steering it into that small piece of the sky from which their bombs would fall to hit their target. A bomber crewman would have a few minutes to check and double-check these actions, and if they got it wrong they would have to go around and make a very dangerous second run. A maritime patrol Bomb Aimer, though, might only have just a few seconds in which to react,

The Air Bomber's station on a Short Stirling. It was cramped and surrounded by the equipment, computers and gadgets of the bomb aimer's trade.

particularly if the target was a rapidly diving U-boat. They would have to observe the target, set the sight and select the right bombs. If they made a mistake there would be no second chance as they lost the submerging U-boat beneath the waves. In both circumstances, they would be very unpopular with the rest of the crew.

AIR GUNNERS

An Air Gunner's task required ceaseless vigilance. They had to keep constant watch for enemy aircraft that could pose a threat, or, on maritime patrols, for the elusive U-boats or other enemy shipping. Warrant Officer Stanislaw Jozefiak found maritime patrols particularly challenging: 'They were monotonous flights indeed, but even more demanding, perhaps, because of that. For it took an immense amount of self-discipline to maintain a constant lookout when for hours, days, weeks, even months on end, there was nothing to see.'

As with other disciplines, air gunnery also progressed greatly during the Second World War. In 1939, the average Gunner had received just four to six weeks' training, and most were from the lowest of ranks, separating them drastically from the rest of their crews. Only in the summer of 1940 was it decided that all aircrew should have at least the rank of Sergeant from then on. By the end of the war, gunnery training was so improved that it took around forty weeks, and included working with gun-laying radars.

For the most part, a Gunner's war would be cold and lonely. Turrets were a rarity at the start of the war, and open gun positions more common;

An Air Gunner in a Fairey Battle light bomber. Such positions were highly vulnerable to both the weather and the enemy.

even by 1945, with enclosed turrets being the norm, gunnery positions were still sometimes open, and all were draughty. They were also spread out around the aircraft, and some (particularly rear turrets) were physically far removed from the rest of the crew. The cramped turrets were usually too small for Gunners to flex their muscles, let alone wear their parachutes. In a case of emergency, they would have to haul themselves into the fuselage of their aircraft and attach their parachute packs before being able to exit the aircraft. In an attack, the Gunner would need to be able to spot the enemy in plenty of time, mentally calculate ranges and angles of deflection, and return fire, all the while giving a running commentary to the pilot and directions to the other Air Gunners.

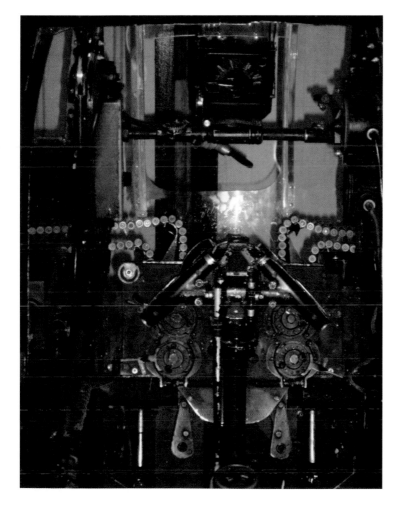

The rear turret of an Avro Lancaster; too cramped to wear a parachute, Air Gunners were freezing cold and isolated from the rest of the crew.

Long-range maritime patrol aircraft could stay airborne for many hours, and facilities had to be made for the crew's comfort. Here, an airman prepares food on a Short Sunderland of No. 10 Squadron RAAF. (IWM CH 418)

WAAF 'Flying Nightingale' nurse Pearl Bradburn tending a wounded Para being evacuated from Normandy. (IWM CL 416)

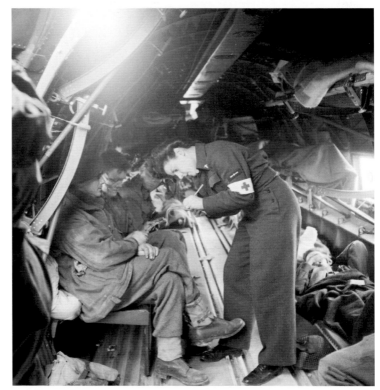

OTHERS

Other aircrew also flew on more obscure types of operations: Meteorology Observers, for example, flew on the high-altitude sorties that swept out from bases all over the world to plot weather systems and provide information for operational planning.

Some nurses of the Women's Auxiliary Air Force also regularly flew, although they did not receive official aircrew status. Known as the 'Flying Nightingales', they crewed the air ambulances that brought casualties back to Britain after the Normandy landings.

Crew rest was also important on long-range maritime patrols. Sergeant Patrick McCombie, No. 10 Squadron RAAF, rests on a Short Sunderland patrol over the Atlantic. (IWM CH 8570)

LIFE AND DEATH

A bomber crew
from No. 35
Squadron
surrounded by
their safety
equipment. As well
as padded 'Sidcott'
suits, sheepskin-
lined leather 'Irvin'
jackets, life jackets
and parachutes,
at the back is
a pigeon basket.
(IWM D 6015)

TOURS

British airmen during the Second World War could face a particularly intensive level of combat. Until the First World War, it was usual for soldiers or sailors, even while on campaign, to see actual fighting only on a handful of days per year. Even during the intensive ground operations of the First and Second World Wars, units were regularly rotated and men were seldom involved in combat, or even in the trenches, for more than a few days at a time. Aircrew, though, could face combat daily, sometimes even several times a day, for weeks or months on end. A system of 'tours' dictated how long a man would stay with a front-line unit, with each tour consisting of

Squadron Leader 'Sandy' Lane of No. 19 Squadron, flanked by Flight Lieutenant 'Farmer' Lawson and Flight Sergeant 'Grumpy' Unwin in September, 1940. The strain of combat is clearly visible on his face. (IWM CH 1366)

a set number of flying hours or individual operations. These varied over time, between theatres, and through the different Commands (see Table 1 overleaf). Their chances of surviving a tour were equally varied.

The shredded upper turret of an Avro Lancaster after an attack by a German night fighter.

TABLE 1: OPERATIONAL TOUR LENGTHS, JULY 1944.

Command	Duty	Operations or hours per tour
Bomber	First tour	30 operations
	Second tour	20 operations
	Pathfinder	45 operations
Fighter	Day fighter	200 hours
	Night fighter	100 hours
	Army co-operation	200 hours
	Photo-reconnaissance	200 hours or 80 operations
Coastal	Flying boats and four-engined landplanes	800 hours
	Two-engined general reconnaissance or meteorology	500 hours
	Photo-reconnaissance	300 hours
	Attack fighter / torpedo bomber	300 hours

After completing a tour, a period of 'rest' would follow. This usually involved training and instructing duties, although being flying instructors could be almost as dangerous as flying operations. In both world wars, pupil pilots were known as 'Huns', the same nickname used for the Germans, as they could kill the instructor just as surely as the enemy could. After a rest of six months or so, the crews would return to operations. For fighter pilots, this pattern could repeat itself for the duration of the war. Squadron Leader Mahindra Singh Pujji, for example, completed five tours on fighters or fighter-bombers: two in Europe, one in Africa, one on the North-West Frontier of India, and the final tour (for which he received the DFC) commanding a squadron in Burma. Bomber crews were generally required to complete two tours, although some kept volunteering to go back on 'ops', probably most famously Wing Commander Guy Gibson, or Group Captain Leonard Cheshire, both of whom would receive the VC.

Experience did not always increase the chances of survival. Norman Hanson flew Vought Corsairs from HMS *Illustrious* in the Pacific:

> Flak was the great leveller. It would send to a sudden, flashing death the experienced and the sprog alike .... The enemy had a seemingly endless supply of flak ammunition and the more aircraft we flew over his islands, the better his practice became .... He never failed to greet us with his withering fire of deceptively slow-climbing balls of red and green as the flak rose to bracket us.

TABLE 2: SURVIVABILITY RATES, NOVEMBER 1942.

Role	Number surviving one tour (%)	Number surviving two tours (%)
Torpedo Bomber	17.5	3
Light Bomber	25.5	6.5
Fighter Reconnaissance	31	9.5
Night Fighter	39	15
Bomber Reconnaissance	42	17.5
Day Fighter	43	18.5
Heavy and Medium Bomber	44	19.5
Light General Reconnaissance: Landplane	45	20
Medium General Reconnaissance: Landplane	56	31.5
Long-range Fighter	59.5	35.5
Sunderland Flying Boat	66	43.5
Heavy General Reconnaissance: Landplane	71	50.5
Catalina Flying Boat	77	60

Famously, only half of all aircrew from Bomber Command survived the war, and at times the casualty rate was significantly higher than this. Shockingly, theirs was not even close to being the most dangerous posting. In December 1942, a highly secret study was completed for the Air Ministry, showing the percentages of crews surviving not only one, but also two tours (see Table 2 above).

SAFETY AND SURVIVAL

Survival equipment during the Second World War showed great advances, although it was still rudimentary in many ways. Aircrew were issued with parachutes, although they could not always wear them in the air. Particularly in bombers and maritime patrol aircraft, there was often no room for the men to wear the bulky parachute packs while at their stations. Instead, they would hang the pack on a nearby bulkhead, ready to be clipped onto the harness they were already wearing if an emergency arose. For Air Gunners, this could mean clambering out of their turrets before fumbling for their packs. In a dark, shuddering aircraft in the heat of battle, this proved impossible all too often. Even if they did get the right clips in place, they would then have to navigate the cramped interior of an aircraft fuselage full of obstructions to the nearest hatch, possibly while the aircraft was falling out of control. In fighters, where the pilot wore his parachute as a seat and it was a seemingly simple case of opening the canopy overhead and falling free, he would still have to contend with possible damage to the canopy inhibiting its movement, fire, explosions and the slipstream into which he was falling blowing him back onto the aircraft.

Survival was not always simply a case of baling out. The RAF frequently operated over water – the North Sea alone saw hundreds of aircraft fall into its freezing waters – and 'ditching' into the sea was always a possibility. All aircrew were supposed to wear a life jacket – known as a 'Mae West' after a particularly voluptuous movie actress of the time – but these were bulky and could be awkward to wear at your station. They were also poorly designed, having a tendency to tip you face-forward in the water. Initially, these were grey in colour, although many aircrew painted them yellow (and the Air Ministry soon followed suit) so that rescue craft could spot them more easily in the water.

The standard-issue flying helmet, goggles and oxygen mask, the only head protection most aircrew had. Notice the whistle on the collar, to be blown to attract attention if the airman was down in the sea.

A fighter pilot in his fighting kit: serge woollen uniform, Mae West life jacket, and leather gauntlets, partly to keep his hands warm but also to protect them should the aircraft catch fire.

While flying at high altitudes, anoxia (oxygen deprivation) was a real threat, and could have fatal consequences if the crewman passed out. These airmen are testing their oxygen masks before an operation. (IWM AUS 2000)

Aircraft did carry dinghies, although to begin with fighters did not. It took some time to develop a dinghy that was small enough when compressed to be slipped underneath the pilot and attached to his parachute harness. This meant that the pilot did not have to worry about remembering to grab

it in an emergency, although the hard package, which they would have to sit on for hours at a time, did lead to an increase in the rate of haemorrhoid cases. Larger aircraft carried multi-person dinghies, which included small amounts of emergency supplies, and sensible crews would regularly practise getting out of their aircraft and into the boat in the few seconds they might have before it sank. Many larger aircraft also carried carrier pigeons. If there had not been time to send a distress signal, a pigeon would be dispatched with the crew's position. Later, hand-cranked radios were also carried.

An extensive system grew up to save ditched crews, with radio beacons, radar, fast launches, flying boats, and even air-dropped wooden lifeboats all being deployed to locate and pick up crews before the sea or the cold could claim them.

Even in the air, keeping alive could be a struggle. Quite apart from the dangers of enemy action, at high altitudes the below-freezing temperatures could lead to frostbite or worse if care was not taken, while a fault in the oxygen supply (condensation freezing and blocking the tubes was a constant worry) could lead to fatal anoxia. Although padded and electrically heated clothing was used, it was far from perfect, particularly in the hundreds-of-miles-an-hour winds that could whistle down fuselages. Additionally, the padded clothing added to the difficulty in moving quickly around the aircraft.

Preparing a Supermarine Spitfire pilot for action: ground crews help the pilot to make sure his parachute, dinghy, oxygen and radio are all properly attached, and his safety straps done up.

STAYING ALIVE

So, how did aircrew face these hazards day after day? For some, it was a straightforward case of optimism. Sometimes it was brought about by the innocence and resilience of youth. Battle of Britain pilot Anthony Bartley recalled: 'In retrospect, I realize how pathetically naïve we were in the supreme confidence of youth which would never countenance any thought or possibility of defeat.' Being aircrew certainly was a young man's game. Aircrew could start operations at the age of eighteen or nineteen, and the average age of Bomber Command crews was just twenty-two. Some believe that youth had its own advantages, in eyesight, reaction times and spirit. Sir Hugh Dowding, who led Fighter Command during the Battle of Britain, believed that fighter units should only be commanded by men over the age of twenty-six in 'exceptional' circumstances.

For others, a mental attitude was developed over time. After beating all odds by finishing two tours in Bomber Command, Flight Sergeant Jack West DFM volunteered in 1945 to join Tiger Force (the heavy bombing force being sent to support the invasion of Japan). He knew that the projected casualty rate for the Force was up to 80 per cent, but, he said: 'I knew it would never happen to me.'

Most aircrew adopted lucky charms and superstitions, and had set routines before an operation (the most common of which was urinating on the tail wheel). For others, religious belief buoyed their hopes, and we should never, in our more cynical age, underestimate the simple motivation of patriotism.

For the majority, though, camaraderie was a driving factor. Crews lived together (within the limits of ranks – officers and non-commissioned officers were separated) and fought together. At a very young age they were thrown together, and during these formative years were thrust through some of the most intensive and emotional experiences of their lives. They formed very close bonds. They depended on each other. Frequently, the biggest motivation was simply to not let your mates down, and not to be seen to be afraid.

FAMILIES

Families could also have an effect. Although the conditions varied over time and between Commands, in the UK at least families could sometimes be

Even on the ground and stationary, fighters were a tight squeeze to get out of.

Religious faith was
a support for
many; here, a
Roman Catholic
Mass is being
celebrated
in Burma.
(IWM CF 394)

very close by. An airman could leave his family in the afternoon, fight in a full-scale battle in the night skies over Germany, and return to his wife and children the next morning. Opinion on how this affected morale was mixed. Some thought that the close support of families helped to stabilise airmen, but some, particularly Sir Arthur Harris, commanding officer of Bomber Command from 1942, saw families as a distraction and tried to keep them away from his stations.

When the airman or airwoman was overseas, or, as was also often the case, when their family lived outside the UK, contact could be maintained by telegrams and letters. The former were expensive and less common,

Front-line
squadrons could
become close-knit
support networks.

but many men, for whom this would be their first time away from home and family, would write often. Letters were sent by sea or air; such was the volume of letters being written that new ways to cope with the sheer tonnage were needed. 'Aerographs' (or 'Airgraphs', or several other titles) were standard forms that airmen could write on. These were then photographed in large batches, and the negatives sent to be developed in the destination country. This way, hundreds of letters could be sent while taking up the space and weight of just a few.

The obvious exceptions to these cases were of course the airmen, and airwomen, who escaped from occupied Europe to join the RAF or their own national air forces in exile. For these people, there would be no direct contact with home until after the war, and little news beyond rumour. In fact, great lengths would be gone to in order to hide the identities of these Allied airmen, keeping their names and even their faces out of the press and official publications for fear that their actions would bring about reprisals against their families.

LETTING OFF STEAM

An important way to cope with the stress of wartime operations was letting off steam. Obviously, smoking, chasing girls and drinking played a prominent role in this, although perhaps to a lesser extent than may be thought. Wartime beer, for example, was much weaker than what we enjoy now, and spirits were in short supply. While a few hardened drinkers would always find a

Relaxing between scrambles: even waiting for combat was highly stressful, and a frame of mind had to be cultivated to be able to rest or sleep, or at least pretend to.

Some of the Allied air forces, especially the Poles, became a byword for letting off steam. In a strange country, cut off completely from their families, many felt they had little to lose, and threw themselves into combat even harder than they threw themselves into recreation.

source somewhere, most men combined drink with high-spirited shenanigans in the mess. Singing, practical jokes and station dances were popular, as were games such a High Cockalorum, a dangerous mixture of leap-frog and British Bulldog, or indoor rugby.

At home, and some stations overseas, regular runs could be made into neighbouring towns to go to the pub, see a show, or otherwise leave the station and the ever-present shadow of duty; it would also allow crew members of different ranks to socialise together. Even at the height of the Battle of Britain Sir Hugh Dowding decreed that every pilot should have at least one 24-hour pass every week, with which they were to get away from their squadron. In some UK locations, and many of those overseas, this simply was not possible due to distance, and efforts were made to provide alternative entertainments. Stations and units often, where possible, formed their own bands, and it was not unusual for units to put on their own plays or shows, particularly around Christmas. Professional shows from groups such as the Entertainments National Service Association (ENSA) or one of the many RAF bands would be a welcome, if rare, treat.

LEAVE

Another way to let off steam, and to keep in touch with families, was through leave. In wartime, this was sporadic due to the necessities of duty. Indeed, anyone posted overseas would expect to serve there for two or three years before being brought home. Any leave they received would be to the rear areas of the theatre in which they served. From the Western Desert, this could mean to Cairo or Alexandria, and from Burma back into India. Equally, those who had travelled from around the Empire, or elsewhere in the free world or from occupied Europe, would have little hope of getting home to see their families before the end of the war.

In the UK, leave would be given to personnel completing training courses, or those either about to go abroad or recently arrived home. Other periods of leave could also be given when requested, including for compassionate reasons. Those commanding officers who could spot the signs would also send anyone who was obviously reaching their limit of endurance on leave for a few weeks, to allow them to recoup; this was a far more common response to 'waverers' than the more notorious course of breaking them in rank and status under the stigma of 'Lacking Moral Fibre'.

ON THE GROUND

R^AF PERSONNEL during the Second World War could be posted to almost
any part of the globe, and certainly to any climate or environment.
Training and specialist equipment was usually fairly minimal beyond medical
lectures (many focusing on venereal diseases), a handbook or two, a more
suitable uniform and a mosquito net. Initiative and improvisation were
usually the orders of the day.

HOME SERVICE
Even Britain could be a thoroughly unpleasant place to serve. The massive
expansion in airfields in the early years of the war, usually in flat and isolated

An airman at rest
in his crude billet
in a Nissen hut.
(IWM CH 1466)

A NAAFI van (in this case paid for by the US-based British War Relief Society) dispenses much-appreciated tea and sandwiches to airmen working on an airfield.

parts of East Anglia and the East Midlands, meant that most stations were exposed and had only basic facilities. Pre-war stations tended to have brick-built messes and barrack blocks, where personnel could live in relative warmth and comfort, but most new-build stations relied on huts, usually the ubiquitous Nissen hut. These varied in size, accommodating anything from seven men up to thirty, but all were cold (ice often formed on the inside of windows) and rudimentary. Flight Lieutenant Phil Tetlow was on a bomber station: 'Nissen huts, all very Spartan, with curved, corrugated-iron walls, a central coke-fired stove, a bare concrete floor, a trestle table, four folding chairs, and beds and lockers for the seven of us.'

In winter, exposed conditions could make life very dangerous for the ground crews. Most aircraft, particularly the larger ones, were kept outside, and had to be serviced and maintained in the open air and exposed to the elements. Just one slip on the icy wing of a Short Stirling or an Avro Lancaster could see the unfortunate mechanic plummeting to earth, or, on rocking a Short Sunderland flying boat, falling into the sea.

Some of the more functional buildings were usually better built: control towers, for example, or the crew rooms and messes. In the messes (with different ones for different ranks) airmen would receive their meals, and possibly have basic recreational facilities. Food was for the most part the same basic rations as civilians, bolstered by the one boon of the traditional bacon and eggs for aircrew on operations.

Stations were self-contained hives of activity, with hundreds or even thousands of personnel of both sexes living, working and relaxing on the site. Workshops, storerooms, medical centres, libraries, briefing rooms and even cinemas were provided. Theoretically, all that was needed for operational and recreational purposes was there. The ubiquitous Navy, Army and Air Force Institute (NAAFI) also provided welcome tea, relaxation, and a valuable outlet to buy extra food.

THE DESERT

The RAF most famously operated in desert conditions in Egypt and Libya, the so-called Western Desert. But they also served in similar environments

Loading 1,000 lb bombs on to an RAF Avro Lancaster, November 1942.

A desert bivouac in Tunisia, 1943. In North Africa and North West Europe, pilots often wore khaki as it was more practical, and to avoid being mistaken for Germans. (IWM TR 830)

in East Africa, Madagascar, South Africa, India and across North Africa. In very few of these huge swathes of land could living in the desert be called pleasant. In North and East Africa, and in the Western Desert, units often operated from advanced landing grounds that were entirely devoid of permanent buildings or facilities. Life was lived under canvas, or in shelters dug into the sand (which contrived to get everywhere). Food was extremely basic; Squadron Leader Mahindra Singh Pujji recalled nearly succumbing to malnutrition. It was also sometimes inappropriate, as 'bully beef' in particular reacted very badly to the heat and became almost inedible, while the flies and sand would coat everything mercilessly.

Flying Officer Fred Henderson served with No. 55 Squadron, Desert Air Force, in 1942:

Conditions were never comfortable; sand, sand everywhere, many kinds of unpleasant insects, and kangaroo rats which delighted in hopping around on the corrugated [iron] roofs of the dugouts made for protection from the frequent visits of enemy night bombers. Penetrating every nook and cranny of the aircraft, the sand was a continual hazard to the ground crews, who performed wonders in keeping most of them serviceable in the appalling conditions which generally prevailed. Life was hard, food was poor, water scarce and very precious, and even sleep was often a luxury –

yet morale was always good and received an occasional boost when, one day, a NAAFI van appeared, like a mirage, along the desert road. Or the time we dug up a cache of tins of evaporated milk which had been buried by retreating Germans.

For long periods, the war in the Western Desert was one of movement. Units could be ordered to change bases every few days (leading to the policy of splitting them in half; part A would move while part B was available for operations, and vice versa) so that there was little opportunity to make a comfortable home. Enemy attack was always a possibility, and airmen were often armed for self defence, while khaki uniforms, as worn by the army, were adopted for camouflage, comfort and practicality.

Health problems were also prevalent. Sores were common: lack of water for washing clothes or bodies could see sand encrusting kit, and rubbing

Locally recruited members of the WAAF in their billets in Egypt. Note the tropical uniforms, and the mosquito nets above the beds. (IWM CM 5165)

through the skin on contact. The heat and sun could cause heat stroke, prickly itch or sunburn, which could easily get infected, while mosquito or spider bites could also carry disease or infection.

THE JUNGLE

The jungles of India, Burma, and elsewhere in South East Asia were equally alien to the average airman, and new skills had to be learnt in order to survive. Heat and sun were again a problem, and many men arriving in India before being posted on through the Far East were sent to acclimatise at the camp at Doolali   a place that became notorious for individuals succumbing to heat- or sun-stroke and behaving strangely. It was frequently a different type of heat, with humidity adding to the discomfort. Although the times of year varied by location, most places went through a cycle of increasingly humid weather until, after weeks of almost unbearable weather, the monsoons would break, and a solid wall of water would hammer down for weeks or months on end. The monsoons would wash out roads, flood camps, submerge airfields, and generally make any type of movement next to impossible. After a few days of blessed relief from the heat, the water would have infused every piece of an airman's kit and started rotting it. Simply drying clothes required a major effort.

A group of airmen outside their bivouac at RAF Seletar, Singapore, just after the end of the war.

As in the Western Desert, jungle airfields were often ad-hoc, advanced landing grounds, with only basic equipment. However, the raw materials of the jungle could at least provide the basics for shelter, ranging from the simple bivouac to a more substantial hut, known as a 'basha'. Frequently, these would be slightly raised off the ground, to prevent flooding, and also to keep some of the more unpleasant creatures of the jungle, particularly snakes and spiders, out as much as possible.

In the forward areas airmen would often be armed for self defence, as the very nature of jungle fighting meant that front lines were vague and it was easy for enemy forces to slip through. Airmen also wore 'jungle greens', the same uniforms as the army, including the famous slouch hat. Wearing this kit was more practical in the jungle; it provided camouflage, and also

Pilots of No. 607 Squadron attempt to cross the monsoon-flooded airfield at Mingaladon, Burma, after returning from strafing Japanese shipping on the Sittang River. (IWM CI 1458)

simplified the supply lines. Huge amounts of the supplies needed on the front lines in Burma and elsewhere were transported by air, as this was simply the quickest way to travel over such long distances, particularly with the monsoons destroying roads. Food and other equipment was basic, and the RAF used the same kit as the army as much as possible, just to simplify the job of moving it all by air.

EUROPE

Europe cannot be easily classified by terrain, and airmen faced radically different conditions and environments depending on where they were, and when. In 1939, an expeditionary force was sent to France and in 1940 another went to Norway. In the latter country, low temperatures and mountains dominated the experiences of most men. Many airfields were snow-bound, and some were even constructed on iced-over lakes. There, as in France, the RAF showed itself to be ill-prepared for expeditionary warfare in both their organisation and their equipment, and the airmen suffered for it. In France, the German invasion of May 1940 saw most of the Allied forces reeling back in disarray, and the RAF (like the other British forces) left huge amounts of equipment behind as they retreated. Most aircraft flew back to the UK within weeks, and were followed by their ground crews, who for the most part were evacuated through the Cherbourg Peninsula.

In 1944, the RAF trained on advanced landing grounds like this one at RAF Newchurch, Kent, before going to France. This meant that the airmen and equipment were much better prepared than in 1940.
(IWM CH 14091)

When the RAF returned to mainland Europe in 1943, through Sicily and Italy, they were generally better prepared. Units were more mobile, supply lines better organised, and the personnel more experienced in living rough. Unfortunately, most of these units came from North Africa, and found themselves almost immediately operating in winter in the Italian hills, where conditions were considerably colder and wetter than those they were used to.

By the time of the landings in Normandy in June 1944, the RAF was even better prepared. Special units were formed and trained specifically to build and operate from forward landing grounds very close to the enemy and with only basic equipment. The Servicing Commandos were taught to fight as well as service aircraft, as their airfields in the opening weeks of the campaign were often within artillery and even sniper range of the Germans. Life was still pretty basic, living under canvas and off tinned rations, but supply and control networks were much more efficient and the whole system better organised. For the most part, everyone knew what they were doing, when and why, and there were no fears of being cut off or left behind as had happened in 1940.

Ground crews struggling to prepare a Supermarine Spitfire from No. 127 Squadron in Holland, December 1944. (IWM CL 1699)

Modern
WONDER
The Pictorial Review
EVERY WEDNESDAY
JUNE 24 1939
2d.
No. 110 Vol. 5

ACROBATICS WITH THE SIGNAL CORPS

LOCOMOTIVES "AT HOME"

BRITISH EMPIRE DEFENCE FORCES

THE FLEET AIR ARM

THEY ALSO SERVED

N OT ALL BRITISH AIRMEN in the Second World War belonged to the RAF.
Several other forces also gave valuable service.

FLEET AIR ARM

Perhaps the most challenging act a pilot can undertake is landing on the deck
of an aircraft carrier. Their runways were tiny decks, which as well as
moving forward could be heaving up and down in 20- or 30-foot waves
and rocking side-to-side. Flying at sea took remarkable skill; even finding
the aircraft carrier in the vast expanse of featureless sea was a navigational
feat. Yet these were the tasks carried out on a daily basis by the aircrews
of the Fleet Air Arm (FAA).

Until 1939, the FAA had been controlled by the RAF. Years of under-
investment left them with aircraft that were mostly antiquated (like the
venerable Fairey Swordfish biplane), or unsuitable, being simply conversions
of landplanes to operate at sea. Later in the war they began to receive
purpose-built American carrier aircraft, although these could still be
extremely dangerous to fly. The Vought Corsair, a mainstay of the FAA in the
Far East, was considered too dangerous to fly from carriers by the US Navy,
although the US Marines did.

Opposite:
In 1939, aircraft
carriers were
small and their
aircraft almost
obsolete. Although
the Fairey
Swordfish pictured
here would
accomplish some
spectacular feats,
they also took
terrible losses.

More modern
aircraft had higher
speeds, making
taking off from
or landing on
carriers even
more dangerous.

With no engines to give power, glider pilots had only limited control over their own fate.

Despite their setbacks, the FAA consistently punched above their weight throughout the war. Aircraft carriers operated all across the world, braving Atlantic storms, Arctic seas and tropical hurricanes as well as enemy threats. Life on board was fairly basic – cramped, noisy and uncomfortable – while flying over the sea was an unforgiving task. The slightest error in navigation or fuel consumption could see an aircraft ditching miles from any help.

ARMY AIR CORPS

The British Army also maintained a small air force from 1942, known as the Army Air Corps. The aircrew came in two categories: Air Observations Post pilots (whose numbers included Major Tetley Tetley-Jones, who introduced the teabag to Britain in the 1950s, and James Doohan, 'Scottie' in the classic *Star Trek*) flew unarmed light aeroplanes low over the front lines, directing artillery fire and scouting the areas immediately in front of the army; and members of the Glider Pilot Regiment, who flew airborne troops in engineless gliders, landing behind enemy lines in the first wave of many invasions and other offensives. Once landed, glider pilots, who were all sergeants or above, were expected to fight as infantry.

Both of these duties were very dangerous, and required a steady nerve. The Glider Pilot Regiment suffered one of the highest casualty rates of any British unit during the war, and after the disaster at Arnhem in September 1944, large numbers of surplus RAF pilots had to be drafted in to bring it up to strength for the invasion of Germany.

AIR TRANSPORT AUXILIARY

The Air Transport Auxiliary (ATA) was formed in December, 1939, to relieve the RAF of the burden of delivering new aircraft. The crews were recruited from qualified pilots who were ineligible for RAF service. For some it was due to age or health, for about 160 because they were women, and for many more because they were foreigners. Some of these were refugees from

Members of the Women's Section, Air Transport Auxiliary, arriving to collect Tiger Moths from the de Havilland factory at Hatfield.

Germany or occupied Europe, but others came from all around the world; eventually nearly thirty different nationalities would be represented.

Theirs was a routine but demanding task, flying new aircraft from factories to RAF units. Only very basic training on each type of aircraft was given, while the aircraft were often unfinished, still needing radios and navigation equipment. In Britain's cloudy and dangerous skies, this proved a real problem, even for the most experienced aircrew. The pioneer aviatrix Amy Johnson was killed when she became lost while ferrying an Avro Anson for the ATA, and she ditched in the Thames Estuary.

Around 1,300 aircrew served with the ATA, delivering aircraft in the UK, and later to northern France. In all, they delivered over 300,000 aircraft, with the remarkable accident rate of just 0.39 per cent.

BOAC

Mention should also be made of the British Overseas Airways Corporation. This nationalised airline, formed from Imperial Airways and British Airways in November 1939, operated unarmed airliners, flown by a mixture of civilian and seconded RAF crews. They maintained air transport routes with allied and neutral countries, often at significant risk. Many were lost, including the flight to Lisbon on 1 June 1943, which was carrying the actor Leslie Howard. Perhaps their most dangerous and important route was the one to Sweden, which was used to transport vital ball-bearings to the UK, as well as scientists, refugees and resistance fighters escaping from occupied Europe, and RAF aircrew who had landed damaged aircraft in Sweden.

THE COST OF WAR

A T THE END of the Second World War, the Royal Air Force and Women's Auxiliary Air Force stood at a combined strength of over one million personnel, operating just over 55,000 aircraft worldwide. The end of the war did not mean the end of their service, though. Enemy territories or liberated countries had to be occupied while civilian governments were established, and particularly in the Far East, where many European colonies were demanding independence, this led to Britain's involvement in some very bloody civil wars on behalf of France and the Netherlands.

Despite their vast responsibilities, Britain's forces began to shrink rapidly. Although fresh stocks of National Servicemen were entering the RAF, it still shrank dramatically in the few years after the war, as hundreds of thousands of personnel were demobilised. This was a complicated process, with 'demob' dates being calculated on the basis of civilian trade, date of enlistment, time spent overseas and number of dependants. Personnel were allocated to numbered groups, and one's demob number became a forces-wide obsession. The system was not always seen to be fair, and in the Far East in

Paul Day's superb sculpture on the Battle of Britain Memorial on London's Victoria Embankment captures the terror of air combat.

Veterans of the Battle of Britain receive the salute at the memorial at Capel-le-Ferne, near Folkestone.

A few of the 7,500 graves at Reichswald Forest War Cemetery, Germany. Most of them are for RAF personnel, and this is just one of several similar sites.

The magnificent Air Forces Memorial at Runnymede records the names of over 20,000 Royal, Allied and Dominion Air Force personnel who were killed in the UK and north and western Europe, and who have no known grave.

particular, there were demonstrations complaining about the system and its slowness. Eventually, though, each person found him- or herself called back to Britain, slowly working their way through one of the vast warehouses where their kit was turned in, paperwork signed, accounts settled, and a set of civilian clothes issued before they were released onto 'Civvy Street'.

Some stayed in the RAF, where permanent posts or commissions were fought over vigorously, and often involved a drop in rank. The RAF was radically refocused in the months after the war, and the fighting arms reduced while non-combat forces were expanded. Many former bomber or maritime patrol crewmembers found themselves operating the transport aircraft that formed the life-blood of large parts of the Commonwealth and occupied territories.

On the outside, civilian work could be hard to find, even for highly trained and experienced specialists such as aircrew. There were simply too many people chasing too few jobs, while many also found the transition to civilian life difficult. For many young men and women, who had enlisted at seventeen, they had never known a life apart from one where food, accommodation and clothing were simply provided, and medical care easily accessible.

Others, of course, struggled for different reasons. Physical and mental wounds took a long time to heal, and for some they never did.

Around 70,000 Royal and Women's Auxiliary Air Force personnel were killed during the Second World War. At the end of the war, over 40,000 of them had no known grave, having in many cases simply taken off for an operation and never been seen again. In previous wars, most notably on the Western Front during the Great War, missing personnel had remained as such, and vast memorials were built to their memory. In 1945, the RAF took a different approach, and the Missing Research and Enquiry Service was formed to attempt to trace every missing person. In Europe, the Far East and Mediterranean, they scoured enemy records and searched the land. By the time they were disbanded in 1952, they had either recovered or otherwise accounted for (that is, positively lost at sea) most of the missing.

Where bodies were found, they were handed over to the Imperial (later Commonwealth) War Graves Commission for burial. Where the bodies could not be recovered, or by 1952 had still not been traced, their names were inscribed on special memorials. The most famous of these is the Air Forces Memorial at Runnymede, although this only covers those who went missing in Europe. Similar memorials record the missing in other theatres at El Alamein, in Singapore, in Karachi, and in Ottawa.

The opening of the Bomber Command Memorial in London's Green Park in June, 2012.

THE RAF:
A BEGINNER'S
GUIDE

SINCE THIS BOOK is largely concerned with the RAF, it may be useful to provide a brief guide to its organisation here.

The basic unit in the RAF is a Squadron, but the size of this unit varied dramatically, consisting of twelve to thirty aircraft, depending on its role,

location and the time in the war. Fighter Squadrons were usually led by Squadron Leaders, and had around twenty pilots and fifteen to twenty aircraft, of which a dozen or so would be serviceable at a time; they would be split into two Flights of six (each usually under a Flight Lieutenant) which were themselves split into two sections.

Bomber and Transport Squadrons were generally larger, and from the middle of the war could consist of two or three Flights of ten aircraft. Due to the larger size (ten aircraft could equal over seventy aircrew) such a Squadron would be led by a Wing Commander and each Flight by a Squadron Leader.

Above a Squadron was usually a Wing, led by a Wing Commander. In the UK, only fighter and tactical reconnaissance units formed Wings, each of between two and six Squadrons, while Bomber Command and Coastal Command usually did not. Most overseas units were also organised into Wings.

Air and ground crews celebrate the hundredth operation of Avro Lancaster R5868 of No. 467 Squadron RAAF in May, 1944. This aircraft is now preserved at the RAF Museum, Hendon, and is the oldest surviving Lancaster. (IWM TR 1795)

Above the Wing was the Group, under a Group Captain; in the UK, Bomber, Coastal and Fighter Commands were all organised into Groups based on their geographical location. This simplified command, with a Group being in charge of all of the Squadrons from that Command in a given area.

Above the Group was the Command. These controlled all of the units of a particular type in the UK in the air (Bomber, Fighter, Coastal, Transport, and so on) and on the ground (Technical Training, Balloon, Maintenance, and so on). Overseas, Commands (or the equivalent units, the Air Force or Tactical Air Force) would control all of the units, regardless of type, in a particular country or region (for example, South East Asia Command, West Africa Command, the Desert Air Force, 2nd Tactical Air Force).

The sizes of these different units and how they related to each other and their superiors varied with time and location. Some quirks also developed, mainly in how Squadrons related to their support staff. Generally, in Britain, Squadrons consisted only of the aircrew, a few administrative staff, and a small number of specialist ground crews for the maintenance of their aircraft. The bulk of the ground staff – mechanics, cooks, clerks – came from the stations from which they were operating. This system did not work so well overseas, where, rather than well-established stations, units often worked from scratch-built airfields or advanced landing ground cut out of the jungle or marked out in the desert. Servicing Echelons and other ground support units were therefore formed and attached to specific Squadrons to follow and maintain them.

At home, as congestion on airfields grew, satellite stations were built. These were known by several different names, and initially were simple runways with basic amenities, which aircraft would disperse to and operate from for the day (principally for training) before returning to their main

Flight Lieutenant William Potter poses with his ground crew and Navigator (far right) in front of their de Havilland Mosquito, No. 107 Squadron, 1944.

base. Later they became more developed, and proper airfields in their own right. To save on manpower and paperwork, command and administration would remain with the parent Station. In Bomber Command, these small clusters of Stations became known as Bases.

Flying Squadrons were supported by hundreds, if not thousands, of non-flying units. We can barely scratch the surface of them here, and they varied greatly. Numerous Group and Command Headquarters provided planning and direction, organised replacement aircraft and crews, and administered the massive quantities of supplies needed to keep their units running. Lower down, specialist units provided for everything from the erection of communication aerials to storage and movement of supplies; from recovery and recycling of wrecked aircraft to the digging of wells. From 1942, the RAF even had its own ground troops for airfield defence: the RAF Regiment, the renowned 'Rock Apes'.

Naturally it was the flying units, who faced the daily dangers of operating in enemy skies, who received the bulk of the attention. But we must never forget the hundreds of thousands of men and women on the ground who successfully struggled despite rationing and shortages, enemy air attack, bad weather and hostile climates, to keep the RAF working, and without whom not a single aircraft would ever have taken off.

Flying (and taking photographs of) fighters required a steady hand and steadier nerves.

PLACES TO VISIT

Brooklands Museum, Brooklands Road, Weybridge, Surrey KT13 0QN.
Telephone: 01932 857381. Website: www.brooklandsmuseum.com
Fleet Air Arm Museum, RNAS Yeovilton, Ilchester, Somerset BA22 8HT.
Telephone: 01935 840565. Website: www.fleetairarm.com
Imperial War Museum Duxford, Cambridgeshire CB22 4QR.
Telephone: 01223 835000. Website: www.iwm.org.uk
Kent Battle of Britain Museum, Aerodrome Road, Hawkinge,
Nr. Folkestone, Kent CT18 7AG. Telephone: 01303 893140.
Website: www.kbobm.org
Lincolnshire Aviation Heritage Centre, East Kirkby Airfield, East Kirkby,
Nr. Spilsby, Lincolnshire PE23 4DE. Telephone: 01790 763207.
Website: www.lincsaviation.co.uk
National Museum of Flight, East Fortune Airfield, East Lothian EH39 5LF.
Telephone: 0300 123 6789. Website: www.nms.ac.uk
Royal Air Force Museum, Grahame Park Way, Hendon, London NW9 5LL.
Telephone: 020 8205 2266. Website: www.rafmuseum.org.uk
Royal Air Force Museum Cosford, Shifnal, Shropshire TF11 8UP.
Telephone: 01902 376200. Website: www.rafmuseum.org.uk
Tangmere Military Aviation Museum, Tangmere, Nr. Chichester, West
Sussex PO20 2ES. Telephone: 01243 790090. Website: www.tangmere-
museum.org.uk

FURTHER READING

Bartley, Anthony. *Smoke Trails in the Sky*. Crecy Publishing, 1997.
Bishop, Patrick. *Fighter Boys: Saving Britain 1940*. Harper Perennial, 2004.
Bishop, Patrick. *Bomber Boys: Fighting Back, 1940–1945*. Harper
Perennial, 2008.
Bowyer, Chaz, and Shores, Christopher. *Desert Air Force at War*.
Littlehampton Book Services, 1981.
Doyle, Peter. *Prisoner of War in Germany*. Shire Publications, 2008.
Escott, Beryl. *The WAAF*. Shire Publications, 2001.
Falconer, Jonathan. *The Bomber Command Handbook, 1939–1945*.
Sutton Publishing, 2002.
Falconer, Jonathan. *RAF Bomber Crewman*. Shire Publications, 2010.
Gibson VC, Guy. *Enemy Coast Ahead*. Goodall Publications, 1998.
Hadaway, Stuart. *Missing Believed Killed: RAF Casualty Policy and the Missing
Research and Enquiry Service, 1939–1952*. Pen & Sword Aviation, 2012.

Hendrie, Andrew. *The Cinderella Service: RAF Coastal Command, 1939–1945*. Pen & Sword Aviation, 2010.

Middlebrook, Martin. *The Bomber Command War Diaries: An Operational Reference Book, 1939–1945*. Midland Publishing, 2011.

Overy, Richard. *Bomber Command, 1939–1945: Reaping the Whirlwind*. Bookmart Ltd, 2000.

Probert, Henry. *The Forgotten Air Force: The RAF in the War against Japan, 1941–1945*. Brassey, 1995.

Terraine, John. *The Right of the Line*. Wordsworth Editions Ltd, 1998.

Turner, John. *The WAAF at War*. Pen & Sword Aviation, 2011.

Wellum, Geoffrey. *First Light*. Penguin, 2009.

Wragg, David. *The Fleet Air Arm Handbook, 1939–1945*. Sutton Publishing, 2003.

Wragg, David. *The Royal Air Force Handbook, 1939–1945*. Sutton Publishing, 2007.

A bomber crew, represented in the sculpture by Philip Jackson in the Bomber Command Memorial, Green Park, London.

INDEX